PIANO • VOCAL • GUITAR   THE **BIG BOOK** OF   3RD EDITION

CONTEMPORARY CHRISTIAN FAVORITES

ISBN 978-1-4234-9898-8

HAL•LEONARD®
CORPORATION
7777 W. BLUEMOUND RD. P.O. BOX 13819 MILWAUKEE, WI 53213

Visit Hal Leonard Online at
www.halleonard.com

CONTENTS

ABBA
(Father)

Words and Music by REBECCA ST. JAMES,
TEDD TJORNHOM and OTTO PRICE

I'm ___ feel-ing like the ea - gle that ris - es,
Run-ning in this race ___ 'til the fin - ish line,

They will soar like ea - gles.

BIG HOUSE

Words and Music by MARK STUART,
BARRY BLAIR, WILL McGINNISS
and BOB HERDMAN

I don't know where you lay your head ___ or where you call ___ your home. ___
I don't know if you got some shel - ter, say, a place ___ to hide. ___

CODA

house. It's my Fa-ther's house. A big, big house with lots and lots ___ of

room; a big, big ta - ble with lots and lots ___ of food; a big, big

yard where we can play ___ foot - ball; a big, big house. It's my Fa-ther's

house. *(Vocal 1st time only)* My Fa-ther's house.

N.C.

Come and go with me __ to my Fa-ther's house. __

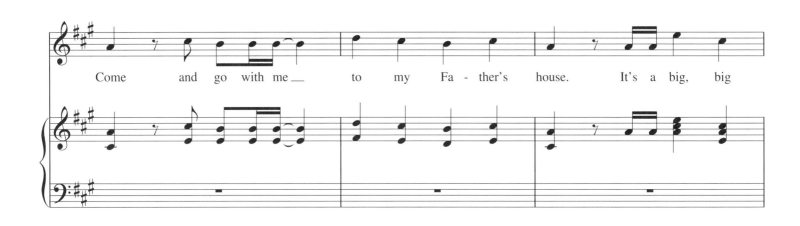

Come and go with me __ to my Fa - ther's house. It's a big, big

house with lots and lots __ of room; __ a big, big ta - ble with lots and lots __ of

food; a big, big yard where we can play __ foot - ball; a big, big

ALL BECAUSE OF JESUS

Words and Music by
STEVE FEE

BETTER THAN A HALLELUJAH

Words and Music by CHAPIN HARTFORD
and SARAH HART

Moderate Ballad

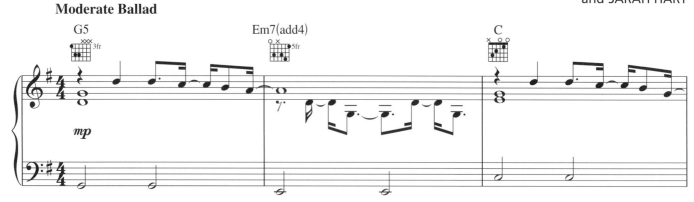

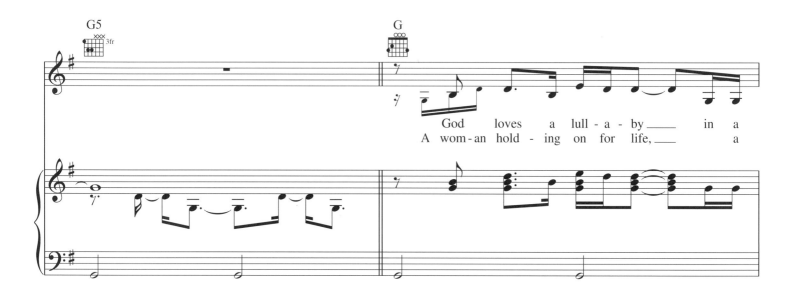

God loves a lull-a-by ___ in a

A wom-an hold-ing on for life, ___ a

moth-er's tears ___ in the dead of night   bet-ter than a hal-le-lu - jah some - times.

dy-ing man ___ giv-ing up the fight,   are bet-ter than a hal-le-lu - jah some - times. ___

CALL ON JESUS

Words and Music by
NICOLE C. MULLEN

CHORUS OF FAITH

Words and Music by PHIL NAISH
and MICHAEL CARD

sing. _____

CODA

Sing - ing _ this song's what

life is _ a - bout, _ and if you _ re - fuse the stones will _ cry out. _ We

do not _ sing that we might be _ more blessed. He loves us with pas - sion,

with - out _ re - gret. He can - not _ love more _ and will not love _

less.

Sing it _ with your life,

DOWN ON MY KNEES

Words and Music by
WAYNE KIRKPATRICK

Rhythmically

I've got a

wit-ness not __ too sta - ble. It would-n't get me ver - y far. __
bit - ter winds __ grow cold - er, they are danc-ing with __ my pride. __

__ I've got __ one hand on the ta - ble and one in the
I've got a chip __ on my shoul - der big - ger than a

cook - ie jar. __ I've got sins that need __ e - vic-
moun - tain - side. __ And these claws of hu - man na -

EVERY MAN

Words and Music by MARK HALL,
NICHOLE NORDEMAN and BERNIE HERMS

EVERYTHING TO ME

Words and Music by SUE SMITH
and CHAD CATES

I want to tell __ the world __ I've found __ a

love that turned __ my life a - round; __ they need ____ to know that they can taste __ and see. __

(Ev - 'ry day __ I pray __

Now ev - 'ry day I'm pray - ing _____ just to

(I'll go to meet You.)

at the end, _____ I'll go to meet _____ You,

say - ing _____ You've _____ been _____ *Male:* ev -

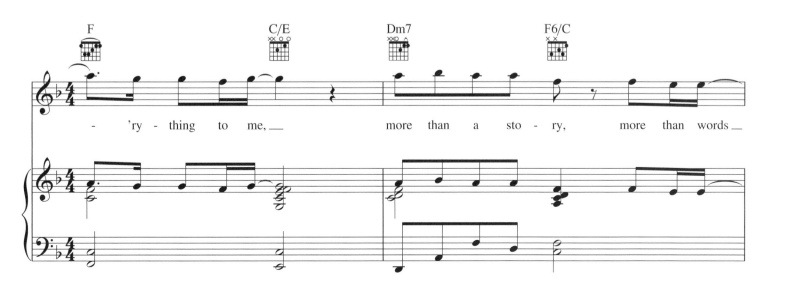

- 'ry - thing to me, _____ more than a sto - ry, more than words _____

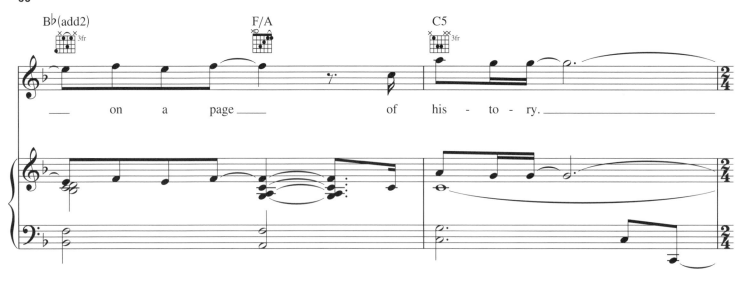

on a page _____ of his - to - ry. _____

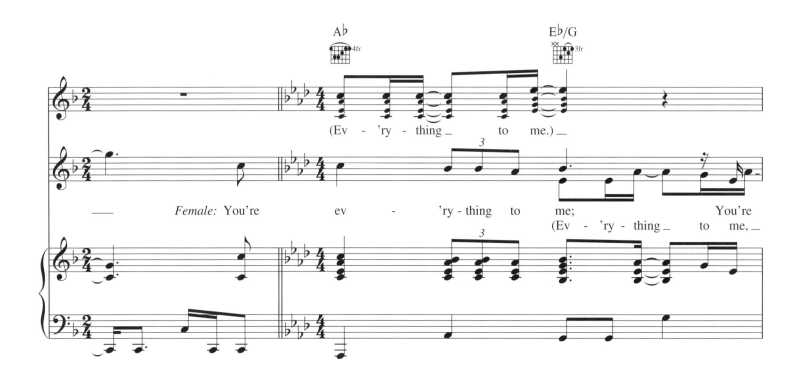

_____ *Female:* You're ev - 'ry - thing to me; You're
(Ev - 'ry - thing _____ to me.) _____
(Ev - 'ry - thing _____ to me, _____

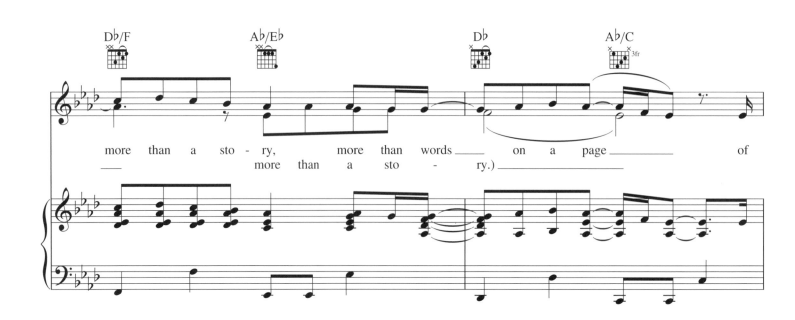

more than a sto - ry, more than words _____ on a page _____ of
_____ more than a sto - ry.) _____

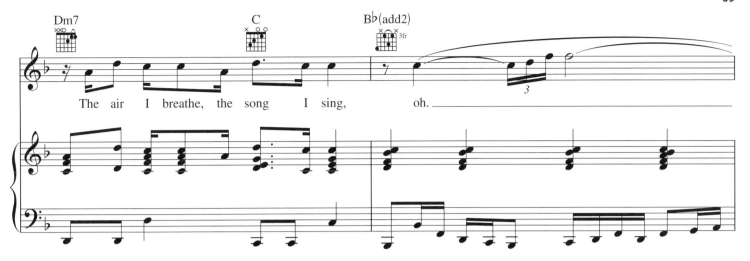

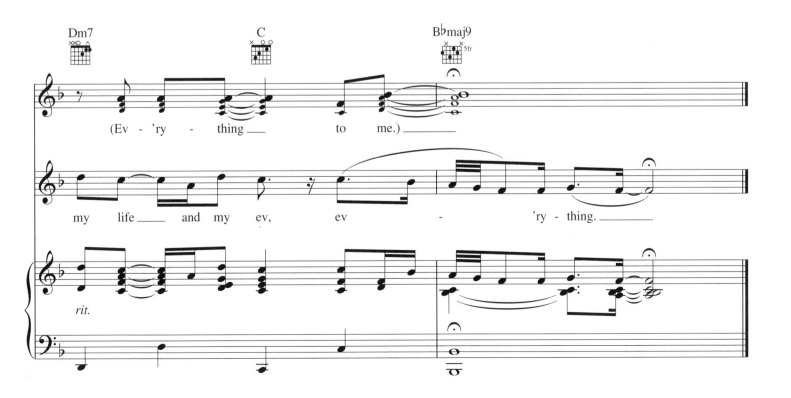

THE FACE OF LOVE

Words and Music by CHRIS ROHMAN,
CHRIS STEVENS, DAN GARTLEY,
MARK GRAALMAN and MATT HAMMITT

Moderate Rock beat

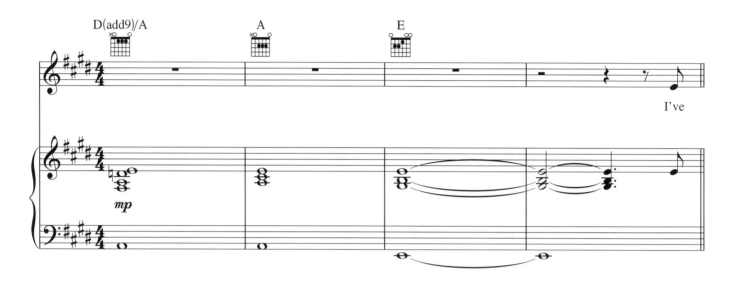

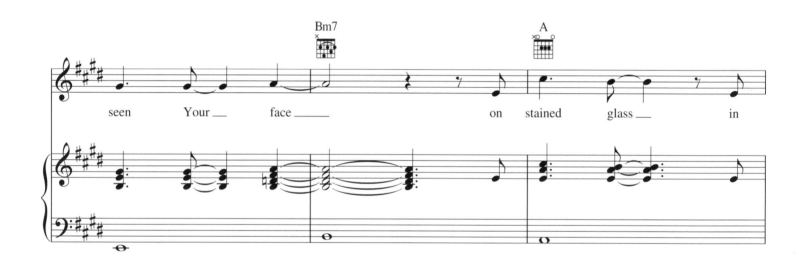

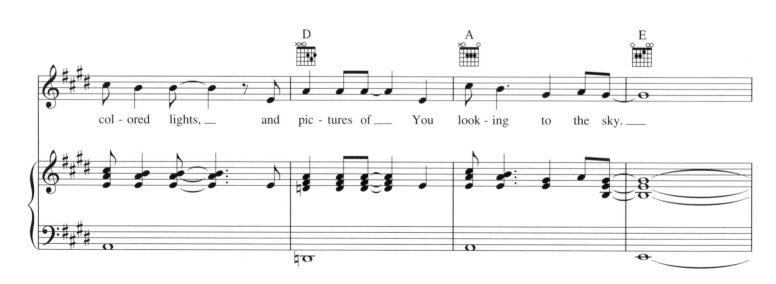

FIND A WAY

Words and Music by MICHAEL W. SMITH
and AMY GRANT

FAITHFUL FRIEND

Words and Music by TWILA PARIS
and STEVEN CURTIS CHAPMAN

FAVORITE SONG OF ALL

Words and Music by
DAN DEAN

Moderately

loves to hear the wind _ sing   as it whis-tles through _ the pines _ on _ moun - tain

loves to hear the an - gels   as they sing, _____ "Ho - ly, ho - ly _ is the

peaks, _____

Lamb." _____

and He

FIND US FAITHFUL

Words and Music by
JON MOHR

pil - grims on ___ the jour - ney of the nar - row road, ___ and

FOLLOW YOU

Words and Music by ED CASH,
LEELAND MOORING and JACK MOORING

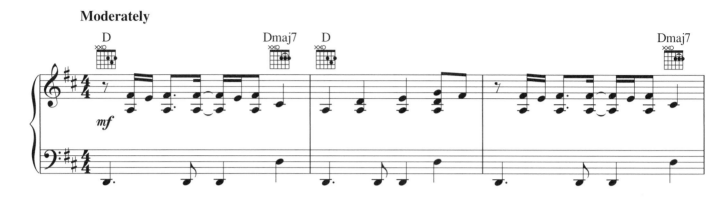

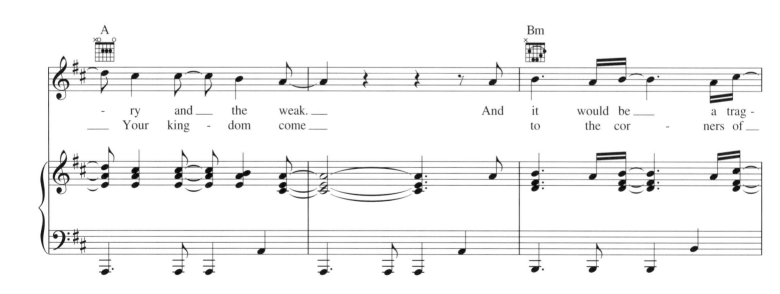

THE GREAT DIVIDE

Words and Music by MATT HUESMANN
and GRANT CUNNINGHAM

Si - lence, trying to fath - om the dis - tance,
faith - ful. On my own I'm un - a - ble.

look - ing out 'cross the can - yon carved by
He found me hope - less, a - lone and sent a

Lord His life has giv - en me mine.

There's a bridge to cross the great di - vide.

There's a cross to bridge the great di - vide.

GREAT IS THE LORD

Words and Music by MICHAEL W. SMITH
and DEBORAH D. SMITH

Great is the Lord, He is ho-ly and just; by His pow-er we trust in His love. _____ Great is the Lord, He is faith-ful and true; by His mer-cy He proves He is love. _____

HE WALKED A MILE

Words and Music by
DAN MUCKALA

Strong Rock beat

fore the ___ threads of time be - gan,   was pre - or - dained a might - y plan: ___
Feet so ___ dust - y, cracked with heat,   but car - ried ___ on by love's heart - beat. ___

HIS EYES

Words and Music by STEVEN CURTIS CHAPMAN
and JAMES ISAAC ELLIOTT

*Recorded a half step higher.

all cre - a - tion __ know I'm here at all? _____ But

then in the si - lence He whis - pers, "My child, I cre - at - ed you, too, _____ and

you're my most pre - cious cre - a - tion. I e - ven gave my Son for

you." And His eyes __ are al - ways _ up - on __ you. His eyes _____ nev - er close _ in

I STILL BELIEVE

Words and Music by
JEREMY CAMP

I'LL BE BELIEVING

Words and Music by GEOFFREY P. THURMAN
and BECKY THURMAN

IF WE'VE EVER NEEDED YOU

Words and Music by MARK HALL
and BERNIE HERMS

IN CHRIST ALONE

Words and Music by DON KOCH
and SHAWN CRAIG

Moderate Pop Ballad

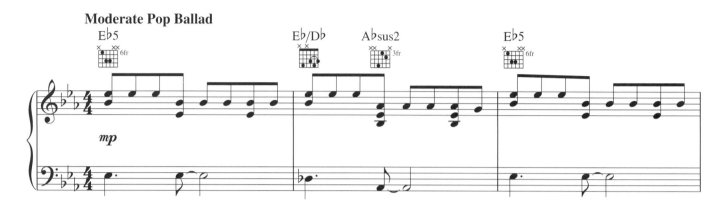

In Christ a - lone _____ will I glo - ry, though
_____ will I glo - ry, for

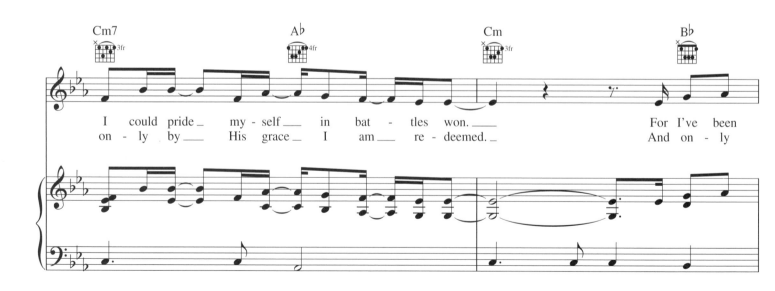

I could pride _ my - self _ in bat - tles won. _____ For I've been
on - ly by _ His grace _ I am _ re - deemed. _____ And on - ly

IN HEAVEN'S EYES

Words and Music by
PHILL McHUGH

JUST ONE

Words and Music by CONNIE HARRINGTON
and JIM COOPER

LIVE THE LIFE

Words and Music by MICHAEL W. SMITH
and BRENT BOURGEOIS

LET US PRAY

Words and Music by
STEVEN CURTIS CHAPMAN

I hear you say __ your heart __ is ach - ing, you've got trou - ble in the mak-
So when we feel __ the Spir - it mov - ing, prompt - ing, prod - ding and be - hoov-

- ing, and you ask __ if I'll __ be pray - ing for __ you, please. __
- ing, there is no __ time to be los - ing; let us pray. __

PRAY

Words and Music by REBECCA ST. JAMES,
MICHAEL QUINLAN and TEDD TJORNHOM

Slowly, very freely

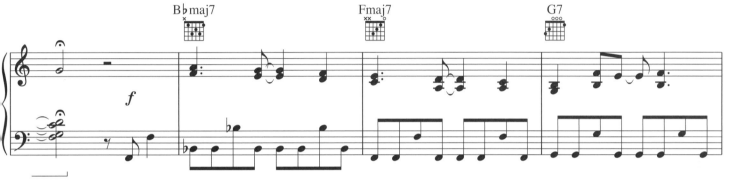

Moderately fast

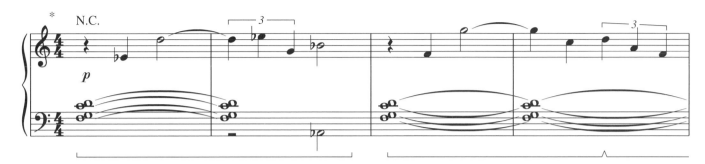

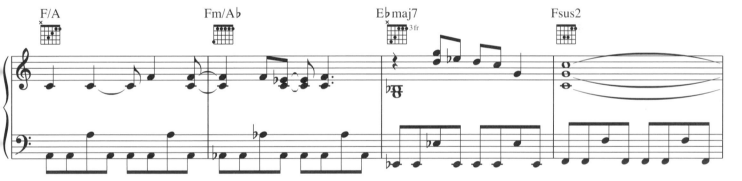

Je - sus,   I am bro - ken now. ___   Be - fore ___

* *Recorded a half step higher.*
** *Vocal line written one octave higher than sung.*

LOVE IN ANY LANGUAGE

Words and Music by JOHN MAYS
and JON MOHR

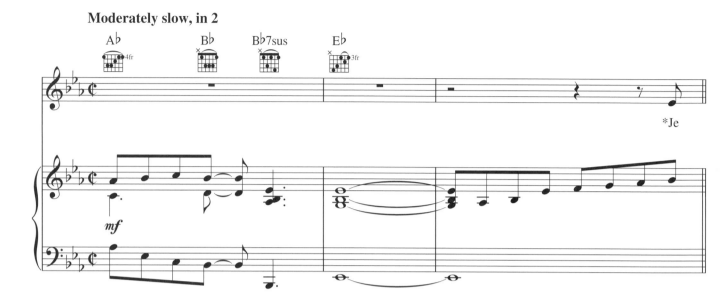

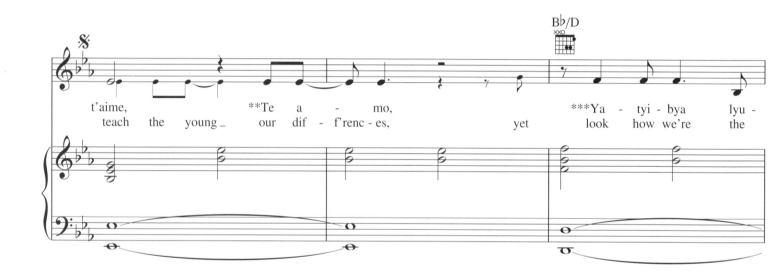

* French   *** Russian (phonetic)
** Spanish   **** Hebrew

LOVE IS HERE

Words and Music by JASON INGRAM,
JASON JAMISON, PHILLIP LaRUE,
MIKE DONEHEY and DREW MIDDLETON

* *Recorded a half step lower.*

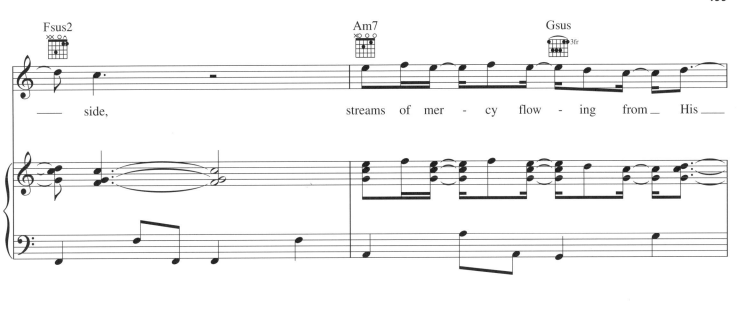

side, streams of mer - cy flow - ing from __ His __

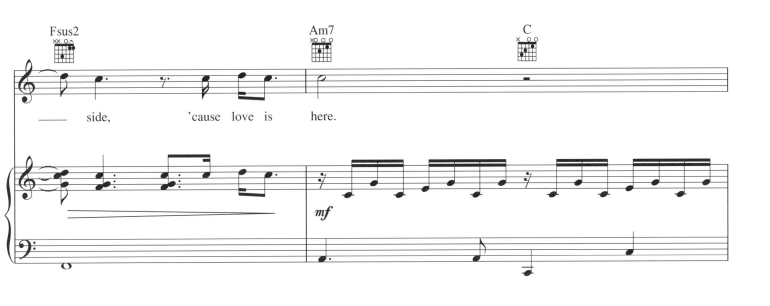

side, 'cause love is here.

Love is here, yeah. __

MORE BEAUTIFUL YOU

Words and Music by JONNY DIAZ
and KATE YORK

To Coda

___ to fill ___ a pur - pose that on - ly you ___ could do, ___ so there could nev - er

be ___ a more beau - ti - ful ___ you.

Lit - tle girl, twen - ty - one, the things that you've al - read - y done; an - y-thing to get a - head. ___ And you

on - ly you __ could do, __ so there could nev - er be a more beau - ti - ful __ you. __

__ There could nev - er be a more beau - ti - ful __ you. __

slight rit.

MY UTMOST FOR HIS HIGHEST

Words and Music by
TWILA PARIS

PEOPLE NEED THE LORD

Words and Music by PHILL McHUGH
and GREG NELSON

Ev -'ry day they pass me by, I can see it
We are called to take His light to a world where

in their eyes; — emp - ty peo - ple filled with care,
wrong seems right. — What could be too great a cost for

head - ed who knows where. On they go through —
shar - ing life with one who's lost? Through His love our ___

REVIVE US, O LORD

Words and Music by CARMAN
and STEVE CAMP

SAVIOR PLEASE

Words and Music by BEN GLOVER
and JOSH WILSON

In a slow 2

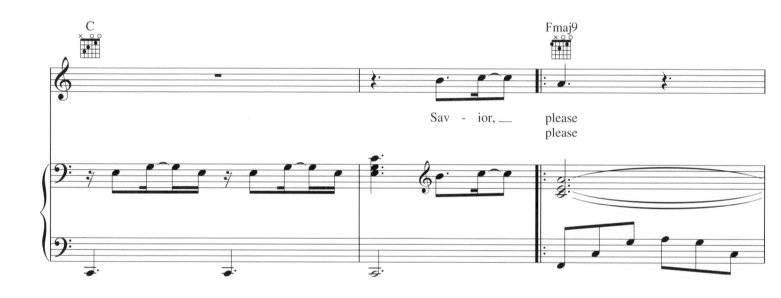

Sav - ior, ___ please
please

take my ___ hand.
help me ___ stand.

I work so ___
I fall so ___

* Recorded a half step lower.

SHINE ON US

Words and Music by MICHAEL W. SMITH
and DEBBIE SMITH

Moderately

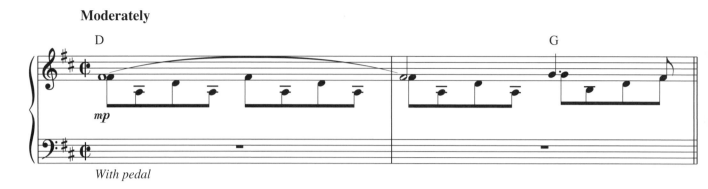

With pedal

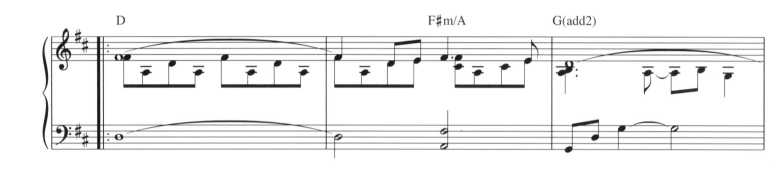

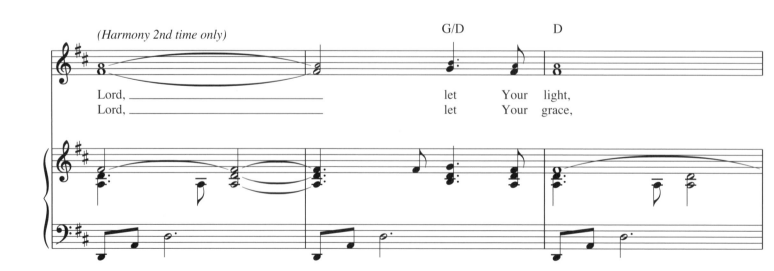

(Harmony 2nd time only)

Lord, _____ let Your light,
Lord, _____ let Your grace,

THIS LOVE

Words and Music by MARGARET BECKER,
CHARLIE PEACOCK and KIP SUMMERS

Rhythmically

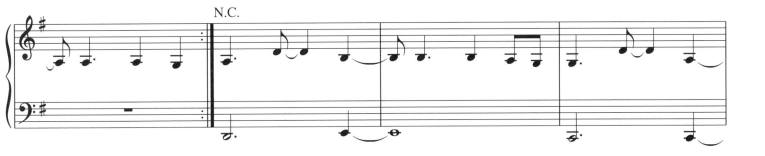

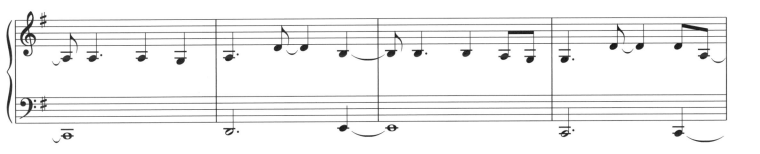

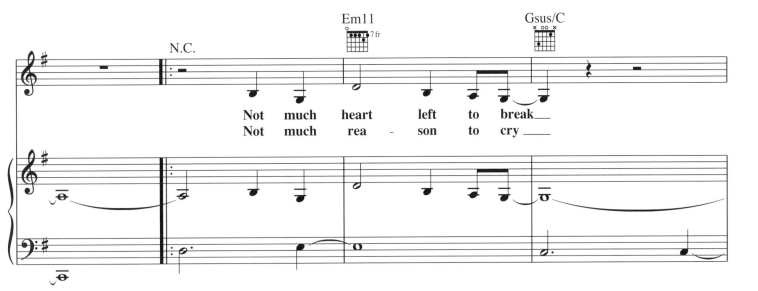

Not much heart left to break___
Not much rea - son to cry ___

SHOW ME YOUR GLORY

Words and Music by MARC BYRD,
MAC POWELL, MARK LEE, BRAD AVERY,
TAI ANDERSON and DAVID CARR

SING, SING, SING

Words and Music by CHRIS TOMLIN,
JESSE REEVES, DANIEL CARSON,
TRAVIS NUNN and MATT GILDER

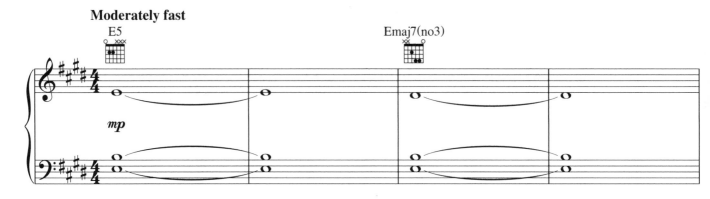

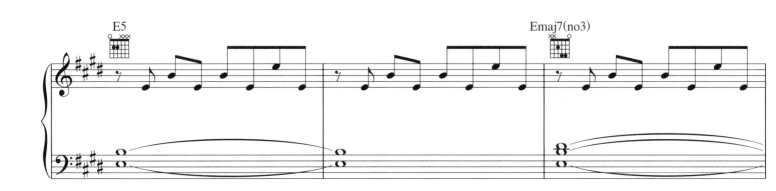

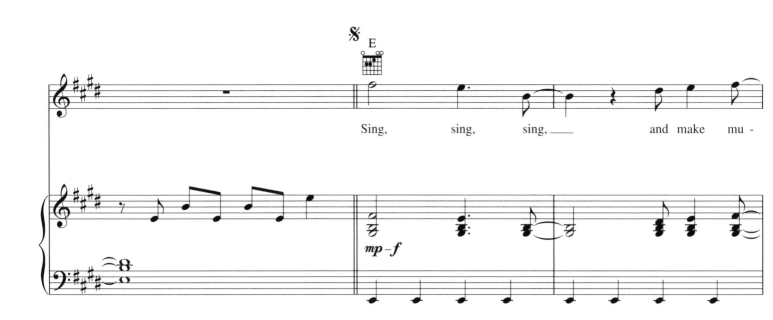

Sing, sing, sing, ___ and make mu-

STAND

Words and Music by LORRAINE FERRO,
TANYA LEAH and JOANNE SONDERLING

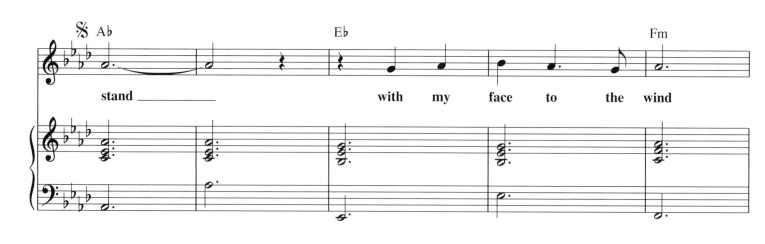

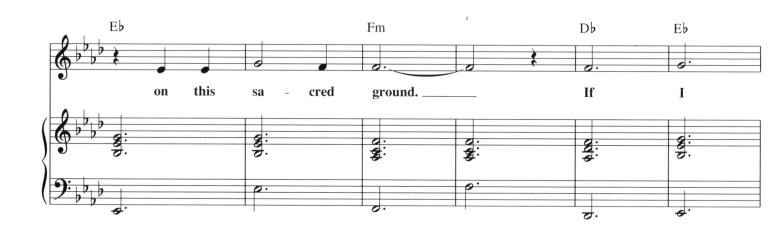

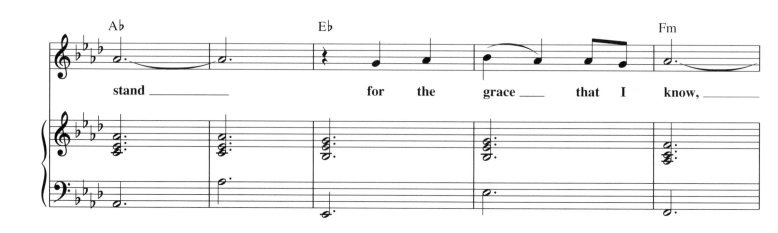

THY WORD

Words and Music by MICHAEL W. SMITH
and AMY GRANT

Please   be near   me to the end. _____
I   will love   You to the end. _____

UNDIVIDED

Words and Music by
MELODIE TUNNEY

Moderately slow

We __ may wor-ship dif-f'rent ways. We __ may

praise Him, and yet spend _____ all of our

days _____ liv-ing life di-vid-ed, _____

TO KNOW YOU

Words and Music by NICHOLE NORDEMAN
and MARK HAMMOND

need to find ___ a place ___ where You and I ___ come face ___ to face.

Thom - as need-ed proof that You ___ had real - ly ris - en
Nic - o - de-mus could not un - der - stand ___ how You could

un - de-feat - ed. When he placed ___ his fin - gers where the
tru - ly free ___ us. He strug-gled with ___ the im - age of a

nails once _ broke Your skin, _ did his faith fi - n'lly be - gin? ____ I've
grown man _ born a - gain. _ We might have been good friends, _ cuz

lied if I've _ de - nied _ the com-mon ground I've shared _ with him. ___ And I,
some-times I ____ still ques - tion, too, how eas - i - ly we come to You. ___ But I,

I real - ly want _ to know _ You.   I

UNTITLED HYMN
(Come to Jesus)

Words and Music by
CHRIS RICE

Slowly, rubato

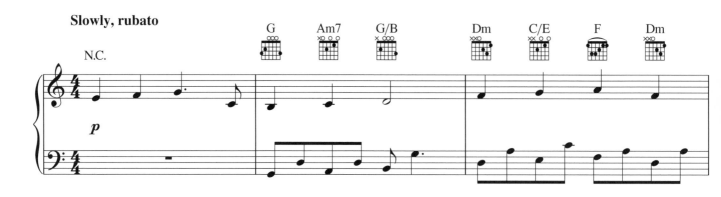

Weak and wound - ed sin - ner,
Now your bur - den's lift - ed and

lost and left __ to die, __ oh, raise your head, __ for Love __ is pass - ing by.
car - ried far __ a - way, __ and pre - cious blood __ has washed __ a - way __ the stain.

WAIT AND SEE

Words and Music by
BRANDON HEATH

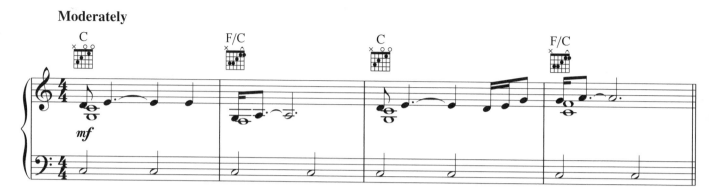

I was born in Ten-nes - see, ____ late Ju - ly hu - mid - i - ty. ____
nev - er real - ly was that good in school. ___ I talked too much, broke the rules.
now's my time to be a man, ___ fol - low my heart as far as I can.

Doc - tor said I was luck - y to be a - live. ____ I've been
Teach - ers thought I was a hope - less fool, al - right. I
No tell - ing where I'm end - ing up ____ to - night. ____ I

WHAT ARE YOU WAITING FOR

Words and Music by BRIDGET BENENATE,
STEVE BOOKER and MATTHEW GERRARD

Moderate Pop beat

Hey, __ yeah, __ yeah. Hey, __ yeah, __ yeah. Hey, __ yeah, __ yeah, yeah. __

Some - times __ I get that o - ver - whelm - ing feel - ing.

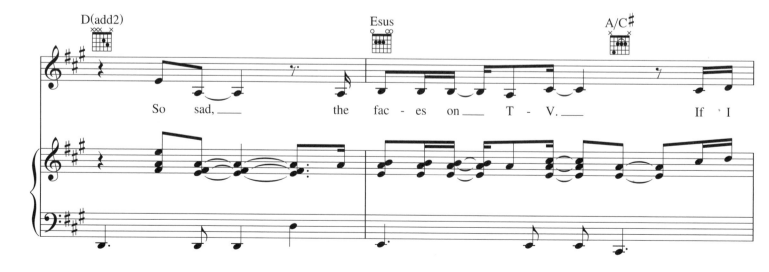

So sad, ___ the fac - es on ___ T - V. ___ If I

WHEN IT'S TIME TO GO

Words and Music by JEFF SILVEY
and BILLY SIMON

WHEN OUR HEARTS SING

Words and Music by MATT BRONLEEWE,
JASON INGRAM, KEVIN HUGULEY
and WES WILLIS

WISDOM

Words and Music by
TWILA PARIS

I see a mul - ti - tude_ of peo - ple,
There is a mo - ment of __ de - ci - sion,